How to Stop Overthinking

Stop Worrying and Be Mentally Tough by Decluttering Your Mind

By: Raymond Henry

© **Copyright 2020 - All rights reserved.**

The contents of this book may not be reproduced, duplicated or transmitted without direct written permission from the author.

Under no circumstances will any legal responsibility or blame be held against the publisher for any reparation, damages, or monetary loss due to the information herein, either directly or indirectly.

<u>Legal Notice:</u>

This book is copyright protected. This is only for personal use. You cannot amend, distribute, sell, use, quote or paraphrase any part or the content within this book without the consent of the author.

<u>Disclaimer Notice:</u>

Please note the information contained within this document is for educational and entertainment purposes only. Every attempt has been made to provide accurate, up to date and reliable complete information. No warranties of any kind are expressed or implied. Readers acknowledge that the author is not engaging in the rendering of legal, financial, medical or professional advice. The content of this book has been derived from various sources. Please consult a licensed professional before attempting any techniques outlined in this book.

By reading this document, the reader agrees that under no circumstances is the author responsible for any losses, direct or indirect, which are incurred as a result of the use of information contained within this document, including, but not limited to, —errors, omissions, or inaccuracies.

Table of Contents

How to Stop Overthinking 1

Introduction 7

Chapter One: Understanding the Problem 11

So, What Is Overthinking? 11

What Is Overthinking A Sign Of? 12

What Is Worrying? 12

Do the Smartest People Overthink? 13

Why Do People Overthink? 14

Negative, Traumatic or Stressful Behavior 14

Passive Behavior 15

How Overthinking Harms You 15

Anxiety 16

Depression 16

Fear 16

Stress 17

Fatigue 17

Indecision 17

Substance Abuse 18

Loneliness 18

Sleeplessness 18

Suicide Risk 19

Signs That You Are an Overthinker 20

Why Should You Stop Overthinking? 21

Overthinking Will Lead to Headaches *21*

You Cannot Decide When You Overthink *22*

You Lose Opportunities *23*

You Will Become Passive *23*

You Cannot Focus Your Mind *24*

You Will Enjoy Life More *24*

Chapter Two: How to Stop Overthinking 26

How Can You Train Your Brain to Stop Overthinking? ... *26*

Other Methods *30*

Chapter Three: Decluttering Mental Clutter 35

Procrastination, Avoidance, and Indecision *35*

Act *36*

Always Keeping Busy *37*

Reacting Negatively to Situations *37*

Brain Drain *39*

Clearing the Mental Chatter *39*

Wasting Time *40*

Avoiding Something That Is Not Avoiding You *40*

Mental and Emotional Baggage *41*

Chapter Four: Clearing Mental Clutter 43

Create a Check List *43*

Remove the Clutter *44*

Work on Your Thinking *45*

Stick to A Schedule *45*

Avoid Technology *45*

Stop Trying to Please Everyone *46*

Live in the Present *46*

Create a Sanctuary *47*

Chapter Five: How to Stop Worrying Less 48

Tips to Stop Worrying *49*

Coping with Worries about Money *53*

Coping with Worries about Love *53*

Coping with Worries about Health *54*

Chapter Six: Removing Junk from Your Life 55

Chapter Seven: Unplugging from Technology 63

Chapter Eight: How to Own Your Mind 73

Step One: Acknowledge and Listen *73*

Step Two: Make Peace with Your Mind *74*

Step Three: Your Thoughts Are Just That – Thoughts *75*

Step Four: Pay Attention to Your Mind *77*

Step Five: Rewire and Retrain Your Brain *78*

Step Six: Self-Compassion *78*

Chapter Nine: How to Stop Negative Self-Talk 80

Conclusion 86

Introduction

People tend to overthink about everything that happens or is said to them. Have you ever been in a situation where someone's words have stung you long after the conversation? Do their words or actions resonate with you like they have woken your spirit up from a rude shock? There are probably many other situations that you have been in, where you were stuck on what was said or done to you. So, stop right now! Do not think about those situations! This is the first sign that you are overthinking.

People tend to overthink because of an emotion, event pardon experience that they may have faced in the past. For example, the characters in the movie 'He is just not that into you' constantly analyze every single thing that happens in their lives. They focus on minute details and over analyze them until they turn themselves crazy. They do this because of some past events. Nicole Kidman's character constantly checks her husband's shelf to ensure that he is not the one who is smoking. Her father passed away because of lung cancer, and she does not want her husband to meet the same end. While she was focusing on whether or not her husband was smoking, he was out having an affair. She missed the signs that were right in front of her because she gave in to her fears. You may also be doing the same thing.

When you overthink or overanalyze the situation, you will lose sight of what is actually happening. Instead, you will focus on how the emotion is making you feel, and you will react in that manner. You will not focus on the present. When you overthink, you will find it difficult to get out of bed every day and deal with daily life. This will lead to depression and anxiety. It is important to remember that your mind is the most important part of your body. This part of your body will impact different parts of your body. Your brain can stimulate every organ in your body and your actions. When you let reckless thoughts wrack your brain, you will react differently. There will be a change in your actions. You do not want this, do you? So, when you notice that your thoughts are trailing away, you should gain control of them. The question, however, is how you are going to do that.

It is never easy to control your thoughts because they are constant. The only time you stop thinking about past events is when you are busy or asleep. Having said that, it will be difficult for you to work or sleep if you overthink. When you constantly focus on one thought, your mind will be paralyzed. It will be hard for you to train your mind to stop thinking negatively. So, what do you do when this happens to you? How will you stop your mind from wandering into the dark areas of your brain? What is it that you can do to control your thoughts?

You will find the answer to all these questions in the book. Before we look at the different strategies, we should first understand the problem. It is only when you understand the problem that you can identify the solution to the problem. You must ensure that you snap out of your thoughts and avoid living in an imaginary world. As mentioned earlier, it is important that you understand the issue. You may wonder why it is not good to overthink when people expect you to think before you react to any situation. It is not bad to think. There are times when you will need to think twice before you act. An action that is followed by overthinking will often lead to deep regrets. This is what we will cover in the book. Read on to find out what you can do to stop overthinking. Over the course of this book, you will gather information on what overthinking is and why it is bad for you. You will also learn about mental clutter and how you can get rid of this clutter. You will learn about what you can do to stop worrying as much as you do.

When you have too much clutter in your life, your mind will be cluttered too. This book will help you understand how you can get rid of that clutter. You will also see what you can do to unplug yourself from technology and how you can stop your mind from thinking negatively at all times. You must understand that you can re-program your brain. This will make it easier for you to stop thinking negatively about everything that happens in your life.

Remember that you are a strong person, and you are not a failure. It is definitely okay to have failed in the past. It is only when you accept these failures that you can start leading the life you were born to live. Make sure that you do not curse yourself for failing. Do not let your thoughts bring you down, because the world around you is already doing that. When you are constantly negative about yourself, you will start reacting badly in any situation. The people you love may distance themselves from you because they do not know what can be done to help you. If you are unsure of what to do, ask for help. There is no harm in reaching out for help. It is only when you do this that you can change the way you think and behave.

Chapter One: Understanding the Problem

When you think too much, you can lead yourself to anxiety or depression. This is something you should definitely not ignore. If you think you overthink or know someone who overthinks, you should read on.

So, What Is Overthinking?

Overthinking is when you painfully ponder over the same issues repeatedly. These issues are some negative events in your past life, and these thoughts will form an endless loop. You will run through the incident in your mind and analyze every little detail in your mind without reaching a solution. Overthinking is not about having many thoughts in mind, but only one thought in your mind repeating in your head like a reel of film. Mind scientists term this as rumination. Rumination is a way in which mammals like giraffes, camels, and cattle digest food. This is also termed as regurgitation. These animals bring up food from their stomachs into their mouth. They will then chew on that food for hours before they swallow it again. An over-thinker does much the same – they pull up some disturbing thoughts and chew on those thoughts in their mind.

What Is Overthinking A Sign Of?

Overthinking is an early symptom and a risk factor for major depression or generalized anxiety disorder. If one tends to overthink for quite some time, it will affect their daily functions or even change their behavior drastically. To avoid further applications, they will need to seek the help of mental health professionals. Overthinking is a common issue in women.

What Is Worrying?

Worrying and overthinking both involve thinking about negative thoughts repeatedly. Worrying, however, is different from overthinking. Overthinking is where you think obsessively about an event that occurred in the past. Worrying, however, is how you think about the potential or about a future event. People who worry are anxious about any futures outcome that may have a negative impact on their lives. When it comes to worrying, people ask themselves these questions repeatedly:

1. What if the right thing does not happen?

2. What if the wrong thing happens?

It is normal for people to worry every day in their lives. Having said that, if they worry too much, it can lead to generalized anxiety disorder. Psychologists and other experts have said that worrying often starts because people have thoughts about thoughts.

Do the Smartest People Overthink?

Most people wonder if Stephen Hawking, Madame Curie, and Albert Einstein overthought when it came to their research. What they did was deliberation. D pondered over something for a long time so they could reach a conscious and careful decision. When they did this, the collaborated with experts around them to expand the knowledge and troubleshoot any issues. They did this so they could reach a conclusion. The keyword here is conclusion. Every expert in the field of politics, business, philosophy of science, will always think to reach a conclusion. It is important to understand that there is a difference between deep thinking and overthinking. The latter will never help you reach any decision.

An over-thinker will always do the thinking on their own. They will never share their thoughts with the people around them to ask for advice. There is a stark difference between an over-thinker and a deep thinker - the former never comes to a conclusion.

Why Do People Overthink?

Research shows that people overthink for the following reasons:

1. Negative, traumatic or stressful behavior from the past

2. Passive behavior developed due to over-controlling parents or relationships

Negative, Traumatic or Stressful Behavior

A stressful event can always worsen or even trigger overthinking. One study found that people who went through stressful situations like serious illnesses or divorce often developed overthinking. The same people, a year later, had developed anxiety and depression. Further research confirms that stressful life events can trigger overthinking. This is also linked with high depression levels later in life.

Passive Behavior

Children often learn how to behave from their parents. When parents depict passive behavior, children often develop a habit of overthinking. Most parents want their kids to do their best in life, and they tend to push them to act in the way they believe is right. They do not allow their kids to learn on their own. A study found that such children were more passive and helpless when the feast stressful or frustrating situations. These children then began to overthink about these events later in life. Another study found that college students began to overthink when their parents control their behavior in college.

How Overthinking Harms You

When you overthink habitually, it will wreck your mind and body in numerous ways. To begin with, an over-thinker sleeps very badly, eats erratically, does not exercise regularly, and lashes out if triggered. These effects will have a harmful effect on your brain. Overthinking has many effects on your body. This section will look at some of the common effects of overthinking.

Anxiety

An over-thinker is always anxious. These people are never able to come to a conclusion about their thoughts. This means that they never know how to react or act in any situation. They develop anxiety because they are unable to help themselves come out of the overthinking pattern.

Depression

An over-thinker always focuses on negative thoughts and mulls on them for hours or days. It is because of this that overthinking can worsen depression. An over-thinker will often focus only on negative memories from the past. It is because of this that they have a very pessimistic outlook on their current situations. They are also very negative about their future. Since women are prone to overthinking, the other ones were most likely to go into depression later in life.

Fear

An over-thinker will reach a point in life when he or she dreads meeting people. They will worry that people will say something that will overload them with new negative thoughts. This can grow into a severe case of agoraphobia or social phobia.

Stress

Stress or distress is a very close companion for an over-thinker. Overthinking does cause stress, and the increase in stress will lead to overthinking. This is an endless loop.

Fatigue

When a hamster is running nonstop on its wheels, its mind will be drained of energy. Soon, its body will be tired too. When their body is under stress, it will produce more cortisol, which is this chest hormone. This can lead to burnout. It is for the same reason that an over-thinker will also be tired. When they constantly think, their minds will be drained of energy. When the brain runs out of energy, it will need to absorb energy from the body that will make the body tired. When the body does this, it will be under stress, because of which it will produce cortisol in excess.

Indecision

An over-thinker will find it very hard to come to a solution to their problems. Even if they do come up with a solution that will work for them, they will question their ability to follow through on that solution. They also do not have the motivation to act on that solution. Experts use the illustrative phrase analysis paralysis to define overthinking.

Substance Abuse

An over-thinker will often abuse substances to cope with stress. Most over-thinkers abuse alcohol since this substance is available easily. An over-thinker will indulge in binge drinking, which means that they will drink continuously for a few hours or days. They may also abuse prescription and non-prescription drugs, other drugs, or smoke more.

Loneliness

Overthinkers often suffer alone and prefer to stay in isolation. They always shun social interactions. They're also very good at repelling other people with their habit of hopping about how terrible their life is all the time.

Sleeplessness

An over-thinker will find it very hard to fall asleep. They cannot shut their thoughts out. Since an over-thinker is constantly running a thought through a loop, it becomes hard for them to keep their body or mind in a state of calm. This makes it very hard for them to go to sleep. It is only when their brains are very tired, and there is absolutely no energy left in their body that they fall asleep.

Suicide Risk

An over-thinker is always self-critical. This means that they are very harsh towards themselves. They have very low willpower as well. These characteristics, when combined with their social isolation and social phobia, increase the risk of suicide. Most thinkers do not seek professional help, even when they abuse drugs. Overthinking also leads to revenge-seeking.

Overthinkers can never avoid thinking about any negative events that may have happened to them in the past. Any thought in an over thinker's mind is damaging. It is for this reason that they suffer helplessly. When an intrusive thought takes fruit in their mind, it becomes hard for them to put that thought out of their mind.

Susan Nolen-Hoeksema who is the author of Eating, Drinking, Overthinking and Women Who Think Too Much, the late founding editor of Annual Review of Clinical Psychology and a researcher in the field of overthinking said that: "People become tired, even annoyed, with overthinkers for continuing to talk about their loss.

They may simply withdraw, or if they can't withdraw, they may eventually blow up at the over-thinker, expressing anger and frustration rather than sympathy and concern."

Signs That You Are an Overthinker

Some signs that you are overthinking are:

1. You always relive an embarrassing moment in your head. You repeat that event in your mind constantly.

2. You have trouble sleeping because your brain will not shut off.

3. You always ask yourself numerous questions that begin with the phrase "what if."

4. You always dissect whatever someone has said to you to understand what they meant.

5. You rehash every conversation that you may have had with people in the past and always think about what you can or should have said.

6. You always relive your mistakes.

7. If someone behaves in a way that does not appeal to you, you will replay it in your mind.

8. You do not pay attention to what is happening around you because you constantly dwell on something that may have happened in the past. You may also be worrying about things that could possibly happen in the future.

9. You constantly worry about things that you do not have any control over.

10. You can never stop thinking about your problems and worries.

Why Should You Stop Overthinking?

By now, you will know if you are an over-thinker. So, why is it important to stop overthinking? It is counterintuitive to stop your brain from thinking, does it not? So, let us look at some points that will explain to you why you should not overthink.

Overthinking Will Lead to Headaches

You do not get a headache when you write something, look for a solution, or plan something. You will, however, get a headache when you repeat the same thought over and over again. When you have thoughts in your head comma, the only person you will be conversing with is yourself. When you discuss the same issue repeatedly, you will get a headache. It will become very hard for you to stop thinking those thoughts. This is what happens to most people. Negative thought or emotion is much like a song. It will repeat itself in your mind until you find a way to remove that thought. When you think about unimportant matters repeatedly, it will only be a waste of energy, time and also give you a headache.

You Cannot Decide When You Overthink

What do you think you can do when you decide to do one thing, but you change your mind immediately? When you work on making a decision, the right way is to think about the problem and the solution for a while. This can help you decide the right course of action under any circumstances. Once you decide, you should follow through on that decision without looking back. If you constantly think about your options, you will only raise doubts. You will change your mind and let worry occupy your mind. This will make it hard for you to act on your decision. When you overthink, it will weaken your ability to decide. This overthinking will lead your mind to raise doubts that will make it hard for you to carry these thoughts out. This type of behavior will waste your time. It will also make you lose confidence in your ability to decide.

You Lose Opportunities

When you are imprisoned by negative emotions and thoughts, you will miss numerous opportunities. When you think constantly, it will put you in a rut. It will be hard for you to see beyond your viewpoint, thoughts, and beliefs. It is only when you get rid of this behavior that you can let different and better thoughts enter your mind. Always become aware of your situation and environment. This is the only way you can recognize your opportunities. When your mind is free from too much thinking, you can see it from a different perspective.

You Will Become Passive

When you start thinking obsessively, you will become a passive person. You will stop taking action and will stop doing things. You cannot make your mind up about anything. You will start allowing every thought to pass your mind, and you will let these thoughts grow, repeat themselves, and form a loop. This will bring more associated and similar thoughts. Remember, every goal that you have in mind will need planning. Once you plan, you should act. When you analyze every thought, constantly fret or keep thinking, you will not get anywhere. You need to learn when you should begin to take action, and when you should stop thinking.

You Cannot Focus Your Mind

When you work, you should always focus on your tasks. Always focus on whatever it is that you need to do, especially when your mind is free and calm. Do not let negative thoughts and emotions creep into your mind. It is only when you have more control on your mind that you can focus better.

You Will Enjoy Life More

It is important that you think about what everything that happens in your life. The only thing you need to do is focus on how much time you spend on those thoughts. It is only when you spend time on your thoughts that you can decide on a solution without changing your mind. This will ensure that you spend your time doing things instead of focusing only on thinking those thoughts. If you do not think constantly, there will be inner peace. If you have inner peace, you can calm your mind since you will become free of thoughts, fears, and worries about the past. When you do this, you will become aware of the present. You will be more aware of the opportunities you have in store for you and will be happier.

Now, do you understand why it is important that you overcome your habit of overthinking? It is not hard to stop overthinking. All you should do is learn how you can do this and follow the techniques mentioned below. You only need to calm your mind down and focus on what goes on in your mind. Spend a few minutes every day to focus on your thoughts. This will help you go far.

Chapter Two: How to Stop Overthinking

If you are sick with your habit of overthinking every single event in your life, you can try these scientifically proven tips. These are effective methods that will help you stop overthinking. These methods, however, acquire a lot of practice. You must ensure that you persevere.

How Can You Train Your Brain to Stop Overthinking?

It is easy to train your mind to stop overthinking by using the following methods:

1. Problem Solving

2. Mindfulness

3. Distraction

4. Thought Box

Problem Solving

Studies show that overthinking will reduce your motivation to solve problems. Some studies show that overthinking is similar to depression in the sense that problem-solving helps them stay stable and prevent negative thoughts from creeping in. So, you must challenge yourself to stop negative thoughts from creeping in and identify a solution to a problem. You must also ensure that these thoughts do not continue in your mind in the form of a loop. Force yourself to come up with the solution to any problem that is playing in your mind. Always challenge yourself to identify ways in which you can solve any issue in hand.

Susan Nolen-Hoeksema states that you can identify a solution to any problem if you can first distract yourself from these negative thoughts. We will cover this later in this chapter. You could always try to distract yourself by exercising, watching a funny video, performing an activity that you love or meditation. This will help you calm your thoughts, thereby helping you find a clear solution to the problem.

Mindfulness

When you practice mindfulness, you can stop overthinking. Mindfulness does not mean that you cut down or suppress any disturbing thoughts. This technique will help you train your mind to accept all your thoughts without placing them in a bucket in your head. Your mind will learn to let these thoughts come and go. An over-thinker who is in a state of mindfulness will not control, reduce, or change their thoughts. They will only learn to let the meddling thoughts come and go. This will reduce the intensity of those thoughts in their mind. Lilisbeth, Perestelo-Perez, a clinical psychologist, studied 11 studies that were conducted on mindfulness. She found that MBCT or Mindfulness-Based Cognitive Therapy would reduce overthinking. The method applied in this treatment helped to control the flow of thoughts and teach the mind to accept those thoughts. These studies showed that the effects of mindfulness lasted for many months after the treatment.

Distraction

When it comes to overthinking, you must ensure that you are aware of your thoughts will stop; it is only when you are aware that you are stepping into the mode of overthinking that you can start distracting yourself. When it comes to overthinking, you will focus on an event that occurred in the past over and over again without identifying a solution. When it comes to distracting yourself, you will need to steal your attention to a neutral thought or a pleasant thought. One study showed that when people were asked to focus on specific objects or geographical locations for eight minutes, they became less depressed. If you do not want to focus on an object or a geographical location, you can distract yourself by performing an activity. You can also leave the place you are in. If you want, you can distract yourself by working on a project or task that will engage your mind will stop you can also listen to an upbeat song and answer in the room or listen to pleasant music and calm your mind.

Thought Box

You should always set aside some time every day to overthink. You can spend 30 minutes to an hour doing this. Make sure that you give yourself this time every day. Set the alarm, so you know when your time starts. Tell yourself that this is the only time you have where you can overthink. You must, however, stop when your timer goes off. You can let your mind go berserk and think about every negative emotion or event that may have happened in your life. Remember that this is the only time you have where you can overthink. Don't control your thoughts or even limit them. The only addition is that you will sit with the writing pad and pen. Always note down the thoughts that are flitting through your mind. You do not have to overdo it and bend down every thought that goes through your mind. Just go easy on yourself and jot down at least one or two thoughts that cross your mind.

You can call this your thought box. You mean now wonder how this is going to help you. Firstly, if you feel like you are slipping into the habit of overthinking at some point during the day, you should remind yourself that you have some time set up later during the day where you can overthink. This will help you stop overthinking then. Secondly, when you write down a few thoughts, you will force your mind to recognize that you have paid attention to that thought and will stop going back there repeatedly.

Other Methods

Now that we have looked at scientific methods let us look at some other techniques that you can use to stop overthinking.

Being Aware

You may have heard people telling you that you can only address a problem when you accept that you have a problem. The same can be said about overthinking. You must be aware of when you are overthinking, so you can stop yourself. Whenever you find yourself doubting your capabilities, feeling anxious or stressed, you should take a step back and look at the situation. Try to look at your surrounding environment to see what is making you react in that way. It is only at that moment of awareness that you will know what it is that you are doing.

Think Positively

Remember that overthinking is often caused by one emotion alone - fear. People tend to focus on all the negatives that can happen in their life in the future. This will paralyze them and stop them from living in the present and staying happy. When you sense that you are spiraling or moving in that direction, make a conscious effort to stop. You must visualize the things that can always go right and try to keep those thoughts at the top of your mind.

Distract Yourself

As mentioned earlier, you should try to distract yourself with positive, healthy, and happy alternatives. You can switch to dancing, meditation, knitting, drawing, painting, learning an instrument, or even exercise when you catch yourself overthinking. When you keep your mind busy, you can stop overthinking.

Change Your Perception

People tend to make an issue or an event bigger and more negative than it actually needs to be. When you catch yourself doing this, you should ask yourself how much this issue would matter to you in the next five months or five years. You do not even have to go that far. Just ask yourself whether this issue will matter to you in the next month. When you change the time frame and ask yourself simple questions, you can stop overthinking.

Accept Imperfection

This is a very hard task to perform. All we want to do is be perfect, find the perfect partner, lead the perfect life, or find the perfect job. This is the worst way to live life, and it is important that you stop now. It is okay to be ambitious, but it is silly to aim for perfection. When you start thinking that everything in your life needs to be perfect, you need to remind yourself that making progress is more important than being perfect. You need to accept your imperfections or anybody else's imperfections without any judgment.

Look at Fear Differently

You may be afraid because you might have failed in the past, or you are scared to try. You may also be over-analyzing your failures. When you do this, you need to remind yourself that just because things did not work in the past, this does not have to be the same now. It is important to remember that a new beginning is a new place to start.

Use A Timer

It is important that you always set yourself a boundary. This is similar to the thought box method mentioned above. Give yourself some time during the day or week to overthink.

You Cannot See the Future

You must remember that nobody can predict the future. All you have now is the present. If you constantly worry about what can happen in the future, you are robbing yourself of the time that you have right now. It is not productive to spend your time worrying about the future. Instead of that, spend that time on activities that will give you happiness and joy.

Accept Yourself

Most people tend to overthink because they believe that they are not good enough. They do not believe that they are working hard enough or are smart enough to achieve their goals. You know that you've given the best of your efforts to complete a specific task. Accept your effort and know that success is sometimes out of your hand. You can only control how you behave or act to complete a task. You cannot control the outcome.

Be Grateful

Remember that you cannot have two conflicting thoughts in your mind at the same time. So, it is important that you spend every moment of your day thinking positively. When you wake up in the morning and right before you go to bed, make a list of everything that you are grateful for. You can also find someone who is willing to support you when you do this. You can also ask that person to make a list of what they are grateful for. You can then compare these lists to see what good things you are around.

Everybody will tend to overthink at some point in their lives. If you develop a system that will help you deal with it, you can what are some of the anxious, negative, and stressful thoughts. You can spend all that time on positive things in your life.

Chapter Three: Decluttering Mental Clutter

Do you constantly overthink? If you do, it means that you have a lot of mental clutter that you need to remove, so you learn to be happy. To do this, you will need to pay attention to your thoughts and curb any self-defeating thoughts or habits that will create chaos, confusion, or even block your mind.

Procrastination, Avoidance, and Indecision

Do you maintain a mental to-do list that overloads your brain, making it hard for you to focus? Are you so indecisive that you are unable to focus on your thoughts or clear your mind?

Procrastination is one of the biggest problems in one's life. This habit will only contribute to a lot of pain and stress. We often wait until the last moment before we sit down to complete the task, and we are overwhelmed by the task because there is too much to do and too little time. This will lead to stress and anxiety. We will then start worrying about how we are going to get the task done in little time. Since people are unable to prioritize tasks, they do not know what they should do and when they should do it. The easiest way to deal with this is to make a list of tasks and prioritize them.

Let us consider the following example: Archie had a list of tasks that he knows he needs to complete over the weekend. He always spent time on those tasks that he could complete that mattered more to him than those that were burdening him. He also tended to forget about those tasks that were high priority, until one day, he would realize that he needed to complete those tasks before he does anything else. This was when he realized that he needed to change his life for the better so he could be more proactive. He then decided to get his life together and avoid procrastinating. This changed his life for the better.

Act

You must act and always do everything that was necessary. Make sure that you do not keep putting things off. You must complete tasks as soon as you can. You will always feel better when you complete a task since you can put it behind you. When you complete your tasks on time, all the nagging thoughts about how you have not completed your work will vanish from your mind and tackle these tasks one by one. You will be healthier and happier for it.

Always Keeping Busy

It is true that we are busy these days because we take on more than we can possibly do. We want to impress our bosses at work or prove to someone, somewhere that we are great at what we do and that we can do a lot more as well. We take up too many tasks upon ourselves that we cannot complete in the stipulated time. This will lead to more pressure, stress, and anxiety.

Betty is a model student and has a tight schedule. If she is late even for one activity, she cannot make it for the other activities in her schedule. She goes to school at 8 AM and packed with classes until she has to work for the school newspaper. She also takes a language class and dance classes so she can include more extracurricular to her profile when she applies to college. She soon began to have panic attacks and seizures because she could no longer take the stress. You must know when it is time to stop. This is the only way you can prevent any panic and stress attacks.

Reacting Negatively to Situations

It is believed that human beings are wired to think negatively, regardless of what the situation may be. If you ask someone about their birthday, they are only going to tell you about the people who forgot to wish them. They will not care about the people who had taken the time out to meet with them. So, what does this say about them? That they are sad people? No, it is the opposite of that. People are not sad; they are only wired to react negatively since this will give negative emotions a chance to come out. This is a terrible way to live life. This will only lead to a lot of mental clutter and will prevent you from leading a happy life.

Cheryl is one person who is always negative about everything in life. She would walk into a place, and you could feel the negativity rolling off her body. She would constantly complain about her work, life, and how her troubles never seemed to end. She craved the attention of people, and if something did not go her way, she would stir up some trouble, so things were the way she wanted them to be. Cheryl did not realize that what she was doing was only causing trouble. She did not realize that her actions made other people start overthinking. The people around her realized that she was creating a hostile environment that made it hard for them to breathe. They decided to cut her out of their lives, and this left her with no friends.

Brain Drain

You must make an effort to clear your mind and remove any obsessive thoughts that overwhelm you. If you do not do this, you will be bogged down with a lot of thoughts that will drain your brain. You must ensure that you give yourself some time and consciously clear your mind of thoughts that are not productive. A lingering thought in your mind can create a depressive atmosphere that will only cause mental anguish.

Clearing the Mental Chatter

Are there some thoughts in your mind that repeat themselves constantly? Does this make it hard for you to accomplish everything that you need to? These thoughts will only drain your energy, and you definitely do not want that. People often pile their plates with too many tasks and responsibilities. They tend to take on too many activities, as mentioned earlier, but they are unable to manage their time well. It is hard to follow the advice, "Just say no" or "Delegate your tasks." You cannot say no to some tasks that people expect you to complete. From the earlier example, what do you think Betty could have said no to? She needs to get schoolwork done, so she cannot say no to that, and she also needs the extra credit so she can get into a good school. She could not possibly say no to those tasks or even delegate them.

Wasting Time

Every single person on the planet is guilty of wasting time. People need to learn when it comes to efficiency. If you have paid attention to your behavior or the behavior of people around you, you know that they will make themselves very busy if they are in a state of avoidance. We fool ourselves into thinking that we have only become busy, and not that we are trying to avoid anything. We give everybody the excuse that we are busy and not avoiding anything. This is a load of nonsense. It is clear that we are not good at convincing ourselves. If you neglect pesky tasks for longer, they will linger in the back of your mind and will nag you until you get around to completing those tasks. Try completing these tasks so you can see how much energy and time you could have saved by completing the task when it needed to be done.

Avoiding Something That Is Not Avoiding You

Yes, you could have a task that you have chosen to work on later and have pushed it to the end of your list. You may have ignored this task for hours, days, weeks, or maybe even months. When you avoid performing these tasks, you will find yourself worrying about things, and this will make the situation a nuisance. Your mind will constantly nag you to tell you about a task that you have not completed. These reminders will lead to a heavy heart, which will affect your overall health.

The best advice that anybody can give you is to avoid avoidance. Don't stress about your indecision; be strong enough to take a leap of faith. All you need to do is take a deep breath and plunge. Your actions do not always have to be successful, but this should not be of any trouble to you. You will learn more about your capabilities when you take the chance and try something new. This is the only way you can evolve.

Mental and Emotional Baggage

We are always victimized by our thoughts. You may have gone through a nasty breakup, a terrible friendship, or an event in your life where your heart was broken. This will leave some traces in your memory because you would not have dealt with the issue at that time. This means that the hurt and pain will come creeping back into your mind. This will make it hard for you to deal with the situation or the pain. You cannot perform the tasks that you need to because you cannot handle what is happening in your life anymore. The only way you can perform to the best of your abilities is to let go of the pain and stress from the past so you can forgive the people who have wronged you and move on.

Jones always let the past come back to haunt him. He would dwell on how life has never given him what he deserved. He became terribly angry about how his parents had left things, especially his dad, because he believed that every issue in his house was his father's fault. This made him bitter about his life, and he could never forgive his father. It was only when Jones realized that this pain was crippling him that he decided to take a stand and forgive his father. He spoke to his father about the issues troubling him, and his father understood where he came from. This was the only way they could heal their relationship.

You can see that mental clutter will only have a negative impact on your life. This clutter will make it hard for you to function since it will only lead to stress and anxiety. The only way you can deal with this clutter is to remove it. We will look at some tips that you can use to remove this clutter from your life in the following chapter.

Chapter Four: Clearing Mental Clutter

As mentioned in the previous chapter, any type of mental clutter will hamper productivity and slow you down. It is only when you identify this clutter, which you can sort and get rid of whatever is holding you back. You can also put your thoughts in separate buckets in your mind. If you have numerous things to do that you are unable to complete, this is a checklist for you. Clear the mental clutter so you can welcome common peace back into your life. It is only without this clatter in your mind that you will become a happier and more productive soul. As mentioned earlier, you should try to focus on one task at a time. Finish that task; take a break, and then move on to the next task. This chapter contains eight strategies that you can use to clear mental clutter. These strategies will help you keep the stress and anxiety at bay.

Create a Check List

You need to maintain a to-do list if you want to be happy. People have a lot of tasks that they need to complete, and it is important that they track the status of those tasks. If you do not have a to-do list, it is time that you start making one now. Remember, this cannot be a mental list but has to be an actual list that you can look at. When you are overwhelmed, you can look at this list and control your scattered tasks and thoughts. When you create a list, you should ensure that you prioritize the tasks on that list. Always tackle those tasks that are very critical. These are the tasks that you never want to do. Having said that, when you pay attention to your thoughts after you complete this task, you will see that you are less worried. Refresh this list of tasks at least twice every day.

Remove the Clutter

Human beings, in general, are hoarders. They never want to get rid of anything that they have bought in the past or have been given. If you have too many things, you will let them pile up on a chair, in your wardrobe, or even in your office. If you look at your house, you will see that there is no place for you to fit anything else. This is not how you should live. Clutter on the outside will lead to clutter in your mind. When your physical space is cluttered, how can you expect your mind to be clutter-free? Therefore, you need to clean your house, wardrobe, bedroom, desk, and office to get some clarity.

Work on Your Thinking

Yes, you may not be the right person to complete some tasks. Having said that, you definitely are the best person to complete or work on specific tasks the voices in your head will tell you that you are not good enough, and this will lead to negative self-talk. This is the worst kind of mental clutter that any human being can have. You must pay attention to such thoughts and stop yourself from thinking them and train your brain only to think positively.

Stick to A Schedule

You must remember that the mind and body connection is one of the strongest connections to have ever existed. A happy mind will keep your body healthy. You must identify healthy ways to beat depression, stress, anxiety, and fear. Maintain a routine where you spend enough time on yourself. Learn to live well; this is the only way you can keep yourself healthy and happy.

Avoid Technology

How do you feel when someone does not respond to you when they should? What happens when you see that someone has read your message on

WhatsApp, but has chosen to not respond to you? Remember, technology only fills your head with useless clutter and noise, and you do not need that. You must make an effort to switch off from technology every now and then. You should especially do this when you wake up in the morning and before you go to bed.

Stop Trying to Please Everyone

It is important to remember that you cannot please everybody in your life. You also do not have to please everybody in your life. You can always say no if there is something that you cannot do or do not want to do. When you accept a task from another person, you will work hard to finish it. This will eat into your time and prevent you from doing other tasks that are more important to you. So, to avoid all this, if you know that you cannot fit someone else's request into your schedule, you should say no.

Live in the Present

The search shows that close to 35,000 thoughts that are unconnected and separate it flip through your mind daily. It is always good to plan in advance. Having said that, don't postpone joy simply because you need to complete all the tasks on your list. Always work. I'm focusing on the present and clear your mind. This is the only way you will live life to the fullest.

Create a Sanctuary

You can always create a space for yourself in your house or outside. You can escape do this place whenever you feel overwhelmed or anxious. You should go to this place only when you need to collect your thoughts, meditate, practice self-talk, or decompress. When you do this, you can clear your mind of any mental clutter.

Chapter Five: How to Stop Worrying Less

As mentioned earlier, worry is different from overthinking, but it not a compassionate emotion. Worry can also lead to overthinking. Worry does not make you thoughtful. It does not help you solve any problem. You may worry about good intentions, but the worry is pointless. It can also be damaging. People often worry a lot in life. This worry will keep you up at night, distract you from conversations or work, and also affect how you treat people around you. This is especially true if you worry about the people who are closest to you. You may worry about:

- Passing your tests

- How you looked at work or in school

- Ensuring you reach work or school on time

- Forgetting to lock the door or switch off the gas

- What did other people think about you?

- Losing something and more

If you pay attention to what is happening in your life, you will notice that the things happening to you are not the things that you are constantly worrying about. You simply waste time and lose sleep on absolutely nothing. When you notice and follow your emotions more, you will realize how fearful you become. If you are tired of living in fear or of losing sleep, look at the suggestions listed in this chapter.

Tips to Stop Worrying

Read A Book

If you constantly worry, it will keep you up a night. Instead of continuing to worry at night, you can choose to do anything else. Instead of turning and tossing around, you can read a book. You can read anything for that matter, even a cookbook. Read until you fall asleep. If you do not like to read, you can make a simple recipe from the cookbook for the following day. You need to understand that your worry is not going to solve your problems but will only keep you from focusing on something else.

Lose Control

When you constantly worry about an event and replay the scenarios in your head, you cannot change the outcome. You need to understand that you can't control everything that happens in your life. It is for this reason that you should acknowledge that you couldn't control everything that you worry about and let these issues go. In simple words, you do not own your worries. Your worries are very different from reality.

Act

When you constantly wonder and wait, it will lead to worry. Instead of asking yourself "What if" questions, you should act immediately. Always do the thing that will improve your situation. This is the only way you can stop worrying.

Speak to Someone

If you are left alone with worry, you will go through a downward spiral. Always let someone know what you are going through. Always trust someone and speak to them. This is the only way you can add some perspective to your thoughts. This is the only way you can prevent spiraling down.

Write It Down

If you do not trust people, you should write your worries down. Always put your worries down on paper since this will allow you to see what these worries are. This will allow you to see what part of your worry is being hyped up, and what part is reality. When you bring these words from your brain to the paper, you can calm the fear and chaos that is in your mind.

Exercise

When you exercise, you can trick your brain into keeping up with your body. You can do jumping jacks, take a brisk walk, dance around the kitchen, turn the tunes up or perform any other activity that will increase your heart rate. This is the only way you can stop your mind from worrying.

Act Like Scarlett O'Hara

Scarlett O'Hara never let her worry bring her down. She always told herself that she would think about the issue tomorrow. Always allow yourself to put your worries off until the following day. The chances are that you will never remember what these worries even are.

Stop Using Google

Before you use Google to understand your next headache or heartache, you should take some time to decide whom you should consult and how you feel. If you do not feel too well and begin to research your symptoms, you will be more worried. You will simply worry. The Internet is a great source to find the right information, but you can always find a negative response to every positive response. This is a helpful result. When you Google search in a panic, it will end badly.

Reflect

Take some time to write down about your last worry session. Ask yourself what you gained by worrying. Try to see how you feel. You need to learn from that and recognize that when you constantly worry, you can either focus on something that matters. You can also focus on something better in your life.

Help Someone

The best way you can stop yourself from thinking about your worries or about yourself is to help someone else.

You can use one or more of these tips to help you cope with worry. When you practice these tips consistently, you will worry less. You can also eliminate another stress layer from your life.

People always have similar worries, especially the big three mentioned earlier – love, money, and health. Let us look at some ways to cope with these worries.

Coping with Worries about Money

You need to take the power that money has over you away from you. Learn new ways to think about money. Remember that money will come and go in your life in unpredictable ways. It is important that you learn how to control money. This is the only way you will be happier. You can look at different books available on the Internet to help you learn more about how you can handle money.

Coping with Worries about Love

Everybody tells you that love is the most important and powerful thing that everybody has. People will worry about being loved, finding love, and losing love. The best way for you to stop worrying about love is to notice that there is love everywhere. You do not only have to find it from one place or one person. If you want to earn more love, you should give love, appreciate the love and notice love. When you meditate, you will learn to open your heart to love. You will also learn about how love will travel in all directions. You also need to acknowledge love when you notice it. For example,

- If your friend comes over to meet you when you are unwell, you should say, "this is love."

- When you watch the sunset, you can say, "this is love."

- If you take some time out to take care of yourself and spend some time alone, say, "this is love."

Coping with Worries about Health

When you worry about your health, it will make you unhealthy. People always worry about the people that they love, and this will make you worried. You should, instead, learn to live healthily regardless of how your situation is. Always make the healthiest choices and make the right decisions. If you are worried about a current condition or a specific diagnosis, you should be proactive and connect with people who are in a similar situation. You can work with a team that you trust, so they work for you. Remember that one healthy habit can change your life for the better.

Chapter Six: Removing Junk from Your Life

As mentioned earlier, you can clear the clutter in your mind when you clear the clutter around you too. The simplest way to do this is to toss everything that you own into a pile of trash and call it a day. There are, however, some things that you should never throw into the trash. You can always use these items later in life. If you want to know how you can get rid of the junk in your house without throwing it all away, read on.

Host a Yard Sale

One of the simplest ways in which you can get rid of anything you do not want to use is to host a yard sale. Place the items out on your lawn or yard with a sign that says "free." Even if people do not take the items immediately, it is the best way to start your efforts. The advantage of doing this is that your stuff is going to someone who is going to use them. The stuff will find a happy home.

Recycle Your Electronics

When you throw electronics into the garbage, they will become toxic. They will also turn the environment toxic because of the chromium, mercury, or lead in them. When you want to get rid of unwanted or old laptops and phones, you should go to a recycling store that accepts electronics. Find a store, like Staples, that will accept the electronics regardless of the condition, brand, or where you purchase them.

Turn Wood to Mulch

If you are working on a home improvement project, you will see that you have a lot of leftover wood at home. If you are not going to use this wood in the future, you should see if you want to use it in your yard. Take the wood to a shop and pass it through a woodchipper. You can transfer the wood into mulch. This will make the soil better by adding more nutrients to it.

Let Old Paint Dry

Remember that you can never leave old paint cans in a garbage can. You need to drop off paint cans with latex at special sites. If you have numerous latex paint cans in your house and you do not want to leave them at a recycling center, you should let the paint dry.

Sell Unwanted Clothing Online

We all buy numerous pairs of clothing online, and we do not wear these clothes all the time. These clothes will pile up, and they will take a lot of space in your closet. There are numerous applications like Depop, Poshmark, and ThreadUp that will allow you to sell your clothes online. Most consignment stores do not want to take unwanted clothing. These applications and websites will allow you to post pictures of the clothes online. These applications and websites will also provide you with a shipping label and online sales that will make the transaction process easier.

Use Ratty Clothes to Clean

You can choose to donate your clothes, but some of these clothes will be worn-out or too torn to be sold or donated. If this is the case, you should transform these clothes into cleaning supplies. You can cut these clothes into smaller pieces and use those pieces as rags. This will save you from making money on paper towels or washcloths. This is an eco-friendly alternative.

Use Ladders as Storage

It is very tricky to figure out how you can get rid of a ladder that is too old to use. You cannot fit this ladder into an average garbage bag. Instead of tossing this ladder out, you can upcycle it. You can hang a ladder on a wall and use it to provide some extra storage. If you love books, you can use this ladder as a bookshelf.

Give Worn Out Towels to Animal Shelters

Numerous charities will accept old towels, and all you need to do is ensure that these towels will maintain a certain standard. If the towels are worn-out and do not meet with certain standards, you can give them to an animal shelter instead. These shelters need blankets and towels to use in kennels.

Help Wildlife with Mascara Wands

You should think twice before you toss the makeup tools. Since the bristles in the wand are very close together, these wands can be used to remove bugs and insects from the feathers and furs of wild animals. North Carolina created a mission called Wands for Wildlife that accepts old mascara wands. They use these wants in the care and treatment of orphaned and injured wildlife. This organization accepts donations in February and October annually.

Donate Books to Schools and Teachers

Public schools and teachers often stock their classrooms with books and necessary supplies using their own money. They do this so they can provide a good learning experience to their students. When it comes to elementary teachers, they buy books to stock the classroom library so they can help their students read. If you want to clear some books out of your collection, you can donate it to a local teacher or public school.

Give Vases to Hospitals

If you want to find a way to get rid of old vases, you should head to the local hospital. Patients always receive a floral bouquet from their loved ones. These arrangements will always need a vase so these bouquets can last through the hospital. There are numerous programs like Random Acts of Flowers that collect vases from houses and sends flowers to patients. You can use this alternative if you do not live close to a local hospital where you can donate.

Drop Off Shoes at a Close Store

If your athletic shoes wear out, then it's simple that another person couldn't use them too. If you cannot donate these shoes, you can drop them off at a brand store like Nike. This company has a

Reuse-A-Shoe program where they take old sneakers, shred them and turn them into something new. They take play-top surface shoes, running tracks, and basketball courts.

Donate Pencils and Pens

If you have too many pens and pencils, you need to find the right place where you can donate them. You can use programs like Right-to-Write where they take used and new pens and pencils to children in developing countries. The mission should be to embrace the notion that a simple deed like gifting a pen or pencil or even recycling them. They believe that the tool can help them change a child's life.

Use Unused Food as Compost

You do not have to waste food at all these days, even if that food is spoiled. The same goes for dead plants too. The United States Environmental Protection Agency states that close to thirty percent of the food that we throw away is yard waste and food scraps. These items can all be composted. When you compost dead plants, food scraps, and spoiled food, you will reduce the quantity of food that you throw in global overfilled landfills. This will reduce the methane released into the air.

Digitize Your Junk Drawer

People will always have some junk in their drawers, especially the kitchen that is filled with receipts, bills, and take-out menus. If you look for a way to clean up the junk in your drawers but do not want to part with them, you can choose to digitize them. You can sign-up, so you receive these bills online. This will turn your receipts into data using numerous applications like Shoeboxed. You can find your favorite restaurant websites and mark them on the application.

Always Carry Plastic Bags

If you have numerous plastic bags at home and you know you will not use them, you can take them to the grocery store. Since the world is now moving to reuse plastic bags, many grocery stores have started to place drop boxes at the entrance to collect those bags. If you do not know where you can take the bags, you can check the online directory of the Plastic Film Recycling Company.

Donate One Item Every Day

If you are still struggling with decluttering, the founder of Becoming Minimalist Joshua Becker says that they should commit to getting rid of at least one item in your house every day. When you do this, you will find it easier to get rid of the junk. If you follow this, you can get rid of 365 items in a year from your house. If you increase the number of items to two every day, you can get rid of 730 items from your house. This is an easy way to clear the clutter.

Chapter Seven: Unplugging from Technology

Technology is a part of everybody's life. We need it to keep in touch with people and to complete work, and there is no other way to go about this. As with all good things, it is important that you moderate your usage. This addiction to technology is not a problem only for our generation, but for every person who uses a laptop or a smartphone. Research shows that the average smartphone user will check his or her device at least 200 times every day. This means that if you stay up for fifteen hours, then you check your phone at least twelve times every hour. People believe that when they multi-task, they can get a lot more done in their private and work life. Is this true, though? So, what is it that you can do to lead a simple life and get everything done?

Technology Will Reduce Productivity

Research shows that when you perform more than one activity at a time, it will make you slower, which means that your efficiency will decrease. When you bury your head inside a screen for a large part of your day, it will wreak havoc on your physical and mental health. Studies show that young adults who use their technology will show the same brain patterns as the people who are addicted to cocaine and alcohol.

DETOX!

It is not easy to get off the grid and also to live without technology. You can, however, learn to cut down on how often you use technology. Remember that you can be a functioning member of society even if you cut down on the use of technology. You can switch off your phone and laptop sometimes without impacting your work or damaging your social life. When you unplug from technology, it does not mean that you are disconnecting from the world.

Unplug Now!

This section lists different ways in which you can detach yourself from different devices on a daily basis. When you do this, you can get more done at work and in your life. You will have enough time to do better in life.

Begin Your Day Well

People tell you that you need to drink a nutrient-packed smoothie and a healthy breakfast to start your day well. So, why not start your day by refreshing your mind? Do not reach for your phone the minute you wake up, instead, focus on yourself and meditate. This is the only way you can boost your brain. Do not answer a single email or even respond to messages until you meditate.

Go Old School

You should go back to an old phone. Avoid using smartphones and switch to a Nokia 33500 if you need to. The battery power of this phone will exceed that of any modern smartphone that is being developed. When you use an old phone, you cannot check your emails, Instagram, or Facebook. You can only respond to essential texts and emails. So, try doing this. This is the only way you can ensure that you do everything you can.

Do More

People often waste their time surfing the Internet. They will spend every minute of their day surfing the Internet if they need to. To avoid doing this, you should spend your time doing something productive. You can arrange meetings during the day or run an accountability system. Always pack your schedule with activities that will nourish you. This is the only way you can ensure that you do not have enough time to surf the Internet between dinner, sleep, and work. You can do this only for a few hours or days, but it will help you detox from needing to be online every second of every day.

Read or Write A Book

People often check emails, messages, or social media when they travel to work or are waiting in line. This is the only way we know how to manage time. These clips, emails, and images are only making you unfocused; instead, carry a book with you. You can also use the Kindle application on your phone or carry a kindle. You can then switch the mobile off. If you do not want to read, turn your phone off and write a book. You can spend an hour or two everyday writing so you can come up with the first draft in a few months. Will you remember having to use Instagram or Facebook, then?

Download an Application

Do you think it is possible to use technology to help you detach from technology? This may seem counter-intuitive, doesn't it? Having said that, if there is a market, there will be an application that a tech company will develop. Tech companies are developing Detach Applications, and these applications will help you block out some applications. These applications will turn your smartphone into a dumb phone for a specific period.

Diet

When you want to lose weight, you will count your activity steps and your calories. You will try to see what it is that you can do to drop a few pounds. So, why don't you do this when you it comes to counting the time you spend on technology? You should always take note of the number of hours you spend checking your email notifications, messages, browse social media, surf the internet, etc. Try and see if you could cut the time you spend on social media by at least ten percent. When you have extra time, you can try to learn a new language or add an exercise class. You can also spend more time with your family.

Take A Break

If you know that you struggle with technology overdose, you need to take a mini-vacation. You can leave your phone at home and go for a walk or do something. This may be a little painful, but it is not the end of the world if you do not post an image of how your day was on Instagram or Facebook. If this is a little hard for you to do, you can go to a health spa or a retreat.

Streamline Your Work

This chapter does not only talk about switching off your technology, but it will also talk about streamlining the way you use technology so it can work for you. People can get in touch with you in different ways – Facebook, WhatsApp, Instagram, emails, messages, and more. They believe that this is the only way they can stay connected with each other and stay ahead in business. In fact, the opposite holds true. It is always a good idea to limit your connectivity. Always ask people to use only one medium to get in touch with you. For instance, your clients will have access to your phone number and email. If they need to make a general inquiry, they will address you via email. Otherwise, they will call you. Make sure you set your boundaries. Leave your status as "Do not disturb" on Skype, switch off notifications from Facebook, and redirect all your messages and emails to one ID. You can also switch off all other applications, so you do not spend too much time looking for messages that are not coming to your phone. You can also try to delete some applications from your phone.

Be More Active

If you see yourself getting caught in the tech haze, especially when you are on the move or have your face buried in your device when you are on your way to a meeting, you should try to change the way you behave. If you use the phone too much when you travel to work or school, you should change your mode of transport. You need to use a mode of transport that will prevent you from using the device. You ride a bicycle or jog to work. You can also travel with a colleague or friend. You need to do whatever it takes for you to stop using your phone.

Leave Work Behind

When you get out of work, you should really leave it. Always activate the "out of office" when you step out of work. Keep a different number for home. Make sure that you never divert any office calls to your personal phone. Also, avoid checking your emails. You can also use an assistant filter on your email box that will only forward important emails to your phone. I am sure you do not have anything so important to deal with that you cannot spend time at home or with your family.

Always Involve Your Friends

When you choose to unplug yourself from technology, you should tell your friends and family about it. You can ask them to keep you in check.

Tell them to call you out if you are writing an email or checking your phone at the dinner table. When you know that they are watching over you and watching out for you, you will stay away from your phone and laptop.

Lock Up Your Stuff

If you cannot trust yourself to keep your hands off of your tech, you should ask your friend or partner to hold onto that gadget for a while. You can give the passwords to them and ask them to keep the phone with them for a specific period. The other thing you can do it work in an environment where there is no Wi-Fi.

Setting A Technology Bedtime

You know that the light that your gadgets emanate will mess your sleeping pattern. Having said that, we all are guilty about looking at our phones before we go to bed. So, you need to set a bedtime for your technology. Experts suggest that you should stop using your phone at least two hours before you go to bed. This will give you enough time to wind down. If you want to do this for the whole family, you should turn the Wi-Fi off and give yourself enough time to play games, talk to each other, or catch up on a movie. It is easier said than done, but you need to stick to it.

Always Schedule 'Free' Time

You can schedule some time every day where you can spend all your time on your phone. You can play games, chat with friends, or even upload pictures on Instagram if you want to. When the timer goes off, you should switch your phone off again. This will ensure that you use your time with technology wisely. If you know that you can use your phone only during some slots, you will learn to prioritize your time well. You will also know when enough is enough.

Always Be in the Moment

Since we need to show the world what it is that we are doing, we no longer live in the moment. We always want to use Instagram to tell the world where we are and what we are doing. Learn to function in the present. Make sure that you are physically in the present. Always live in the moment – go for a walk to the park. Do not use Google maps. If you live in the city, you can go on a tube ride or a random train. Make sure that you do not schedule the trip on the application. Leave a note on the kitchen table and let your partner know what your plan is.

Switch Off

You can do many things to get offline, but if you think about it, all you need to do is switch off. Make sure you turn off your devices instead of simply using a screen saver. Make sure that you never rush to answer calls or messages and let them go to voicemail and check your messages after every 3-4 hours. Build a routine and stay offline for the rest of the day and learn to enjoy your life and relax.

Chapter Eight: How to Own Your Mind

When you overthink, you often let negative thoughts and events cloud your mind. You may have always tried to control these thoughts at one time or another. You can use self-help books to try to control your thoughts and think positively. The tips mentioned in those books would have worked for some time, but you will see that you are back to where you started in no time. There is an easier way to control your mind – you should become the CEO of your mind. Direct your thoughts to live in harmony with your spirit, self, and body. The steps mentioned in this chapter will help you master your mind in no time.

Step One: Acknowledge and Listen

Every leader is required to listen to their employees. They should listen to whatever problems they may have and see how they can help them overcome those issues. Minds are very much like people. You can calm your mind down and let go of thoughts that do not help you. Always practice being gracious and always thank your mind for its contribution. Repeat the following to your mind:

- Thank you, mind, for letting me know that I need to succeed in meeting my targets, so I do not get fired

- Thank you for telling me that these situations are the most important parts of my life and that I need to take advantage of these situations

- Thank you for making me cautious about the steps I take to achieve my goals

Make sure to listen to your mind and acknowledge everything that your mind tells you.

Step Two: Make Peace with Your Mind

People do not like the way their minds think, and you may be one such person. You may not like how the mind conducts itself. The negativity will also get very irritating. The fact is that you are stuck with the negativity. You cannot remove it from your mind. Dr. Russ Harris, in the book 'The Happiness Trap,' tries to illustrate how the mind deals with negative thoughts using the example of Palestinians and Israelis. The people in these countries are enemies, and they do not like each other. Having said that, they need to live with each other. Whenever one of the countries wages war against the other, the other side will retaliate. When they do this, people in the countries will get hurt. Buildings will be destroyed. If this happens, they will not have too much energy to focus on building societies in the country. If these countries were to live in peace, the leaders could build healthier societies. This is the only way you can deal with the negativity in your mind. You need to accept that you will have some negative thoughts and emotions. Remember that you cannot control these thoughts and emotions at all times. This is the only way you can move ahead in life and focus on the present. You never have to accept these thoughts or agree with them. All you need to do is let them in the back of your mind. This is the only way you can go out and get all your tasks done.

Step Three: Your Thoughts Are Just That – Thoughts

We cannot see the way our minds work. Your mind is simply a part of you. The founder of Acceptance and Commitment Therapy, Dr. Steve Hayes, used the concept of the thoughts being fused together to help you understand this relationship. When he said that the thoughts were fused together, it means that the thoughts were all stuck together. It is hard to differentiate between these thoughts. You will feel like your feelings and thoughts define you. So, you accept these thoughts and feelings unconditionally without looking at them. "My mind is telling me that I am a failure, so this must be true. I probably am a failure. This is very nice, isn't it? I feel wonderful." This is the type of logic that prevails since we are unable to look at our minds. We cannot step outside of ourselves or get a third perspective of how the brain works.

In reality, your thoughts are mental events that pass through your mind. These thoughts are influenced by your physical health, sex, hormones, moods, states of tiredness and hunger, what you watched on TV last night, weather, what you learned as a child, what you ate for dinner, and so much more. These are like mental habits, and these habits can be both unhealthy and healthy. It will take time for you to change these habits as well. You cannot expect a couch potato to stop watching TV and run a marathon. In the same way, you cannot turn off your negative emotions or thoughts without putting in some considerable effort. Even then, your amygdala will focus only on the negative stuff.

Step Four: Pay Attention to Your Mind

The phrase "know thine enemy" is applicable to the relationship you share with your mind. A good leader will spend a lot of time walking through the office and spend some time with the employees to understand them better. In the same way, you need to spend some time to learn more about how your mind will work. You can call this quiet time, meditation, or mindfulness. The amount of time you spend with understanding your mind is as important as the time you spend on exercise. When you focus your thoughts and emotions based on the rhythm of your breath, you know that it will wander. Your mind will bring up unsolved problems and old worries from the day or the past. If you leave these thoughts unchecked, it will make your worry and fear the situation.

As read earlier, mindfulness does not only involve trying to identify where your mind wanders. This method will help you focus on the thoughts that will allow you to focus better on your breathing. If you continue to be mindful for months or years, you can train your amygdala to focus on positive thoughts. This will give you the power to learn when your thoughts spin out of control. You can then guide them back using the tips mentioned in this chapter. If your mind takes off on its own, you should remind yourself that your mind is an integral part of you.

Step Five: Rewire and Retrain Your Brain

People are what they repeatedly do, or people become what they think. Over the years, your thinking pattern will be etched into your brain. These patterns will be etched into the neurons that are in your brain. These thoughts will connect them together in a unique manner if you repeat certain pathways continuously, the neurons will begin to transmit all fire information in that manner only. It is true that autopilot is a great tool in cars, but not far emotional functioning. For instance, you may have a fear of getting close to the people because you have had your heart broken multiple times. If you need to learn to love, you should become aware of this negative sequence and focus your mind on the present. You can change the fighting of the neurons in your brain so you can influence the way you think.

Step Six: Self-Compassion

People often judge their emotions or feelings when a thought or an event crosses their mind. When you do this, you are not showing yourself any compassion. You must remember that your emotions and feelings are valuable sources of information. These feelings will help you understand what matters most to you. Instead of criticizing yourself, you should identify new ways to support these emotions and thoughts. You can seek inner and outer experiences to bring you comfort and joy. It is only when you connect with the required resources that you can learn to navigate these difficult emotions and feelings. This will help you stay in the present.

Chapter Nine: How to Stop Negative Self-Talk

Life is already filled with numerous obstacles, and these obstacles are all outside your control. The circumstances that you are born into, the emergencies you are not prepared for, and the events that are unforeseen are some obstacles that you cannot control. You can, however, control your thoughts and how you care for yourself. There are numerous obstacles that you need to face in the world, so why should you make it difficult for yourself by inflicting more pain? All you need to do is give yourself a break from all the negative thoughts that cross your mind. Negative thoughts and emotions will always do untold damage. This damage can either be visible or invisible. It is for this reason that you need to keep these to a minimum. It is very difficult to do this, but there are different methods in which you can stop negative thoughts and self-talk.

Breathe

When people have failed recently, they will develop a fear of failing. They will continue to beat themselves up because they think they will continue to fail. They will feel bad about themselves because they are overwhelmed. When this happens, you should take a deep breath and slow your beating heart. Calm your mind down; this is when you can clearly see what you are doing to yourself. If you think negatively, you will be overwhelmed. When you do this, you should pause and take a breath.

Acknowledge It

If you notice that your thoughts are starting to spiral, you should prevent yourself from succumbing to these negative thoughts and emotions. You should, instead, acknowledge those thoughts. You cannot ignore negative thoughts and expect them to go away. Most people have negative thoughts when they are afraid. It is very hard to admit that you have doubts about yourself. You can, however, never put these thoughts to rest if you do not acknowledge your fears.

Identify the Cause

Everybody will have negative thoughts and emotions. You need to identify the root of those thoughts. Are you scared? Do you constantly doubt yourself? Did you recently fail? Is it because of these failures that you have negative thoughts creeping in? You should spend some time and try to understand where these thoughts come from and why they come. You need to assuage your fears if you are afraid. The chances are that these fears are only in your head. When you experience self-doubt, you should let yourself know that everybody will fail at some point in life. The only way you can prove to yourself that you are not a failure is to start working towards a goal. Always identify the cause of the problem so you can address the issue immediately.

Never Expect Perfection

Since you are only beginning, you cannot expect to be perfect. If you have failed and you are starting over now, suffering from self-doubt, or are scared about failing, you should tell yourself that it is perfectly okay to fail. It is only when you embrace these flaws and failures that you will move ahead in life despite them. You will become more self-confident and happier. It is absolutely okay to make mistakes, but you should get back onto the track immediately.

Stay Positive

You should always surround yourself with positive energy. This will motivate you to do better in life. You can put on a playlist that will keep you moving, play a podcast, watch a YouTube video, listen to a life coach, speaker or writer, watch a movie that will inspire you, call friends or family members who will know what to say when you are having a bad day or exercise. If you feel down, you should ensure that you raise yourself up. You must always know how to improve your mindset or mood. This is the only way you can change it. Make sure that your thoughts never go out of control. It is only when you do this that you will identify the steps that you need to take to change the way you think and act.

Build a Routine

When you create a routine, you do not have to think too much about what to do during the day. This means that you need to expend very little energy. The easiest way to get rid of negative thoughts is to work through those thoughts. It is always easier to work through these thoughts if you plan your day in advance. When you do this, you do not have to think too much about how to start your day. You will wake up at the same time every single day and wonder what it is you will do next. All you need to do is exercise at the same time every day. You know when it is that you need to walk out of the door to go to work. This will mean that you are not going to overthink anything and will not be stuck inside your head. When you treat everything you do as an appointment, you will definitely rise to the occasion every day. When you suffer from fear or self-doubt, a routine will help you get on in life in spite of them. So, build a routine that will help you get your day started. Try to put all your negative thoughts aside.

Silence Those Thoughts

It is going to be difficult to silence negative thoughts. These thoughts and voices will always want to creep into your mind. It is also hard for you to ignore what these thoughts are saying. You have to, however, confront them. Always create a counter-narrative to everything that is being said in your head. If you feel like you cannot breathe and constantly doubt yourself, all you need to do is breathe, surround yourself with positivity and remind yourself that you are doing better.

Conclusion

Overthinking is just thinking, is it not? Having said that, overthinking will cause a lot of mental and physical problems. When you start to overthink, your judgment will get cloudy. Your stress levels will become elevated. You will begin to spend too much time dwelling on negative things in your life, and this negativity will make it hard for you to act.

Overthinking does not start overnight. It always starts with one worrying thought. When you dwell on the same thought for hours, days, weeks or months it will lead to more worrying thoughts that will make it hard for you to focus on anything else. Before you know it, there will be a million thoughts on the same issue flowing through your mind. If you are in a relationship and have been hurt in the past, you may ask yourself the following questions:

- Is he cheating on me?
- Does he truly love me?
- Am I beautiful enough for him?
- Has he thought of other women while he was with me?
- Am I enough for him?
- What if he connects better with someone else?

- What if he likes the attention he gets from other people?
- What if I am not good enough?

And many more questions. Do you think it is fair for you to ask these questions about a guy you are in a relationship with now? Yes, you were hurt in the past, but do you think it is right to believe that this person will behave in the same way with you? You cannot do that because you would not like it if someone behaved in this manner with you. The same goes for a conversation that you may have had in the past. Remember that you cannot go back in time to change what you said or did. So, why worry about it now?

The only reason you do this is because you suppress your thoughts. What most people do not understand is that these suppressed thoughts will manifest themselves in your mind. These thoughts will deepen, and when they pass through your mind, you will begin to think about them repeatedly. This does not help you in any way. So, what can you do to stop these thoughts from affecting your psyche? According to Western psychology and Buddhism, you need to learn to accept these thoughts so you can reframe these thoughts. You can reframe your thoughts only when you accept them.

A recent study conducted in the UK showed that people who always focused on negative events had trouble with living in the present. These people were always unhappy and developed common mental health issues. So, how do you think you can stop this vicious cycle? You will find all this information in this book. This book will help you understand how you can become the master of your mind. It is only when you control your thoughts that you can change the way you think. You may wonder what you can do to control these thoughts. There are some simple tricks you can use to control these thoughts. This book covers scientifically proven tips you can use to control your thoughts. The book not only gives you tips, but also sheds some light on what overthinking is and how different it is from worrying. You can use the different tips and tricks mentioned in the book to help you cope with negative thoughts, overthinking and worrying. People overthink and worry because of mental clutter. They have hundreds of thousands of thoughts running through their mind, and not all these thoughts are happy thoughts. It is important that you get rid of this clutter. You will gather some tips on how you can get rid of both physical and mental clutter.

Remember, your thoughts will define your happiness and actions. If you constantly worry about what happened in the past or what can happen in the future, you will remain unhappy. Having said that, people tend to overthink whenever their minds are idle. They can think about absolutely anything in their lives. To avoid doing this, you need to set some time aside every day where you only think about these thoughts. Allow them to flood your mind, but pay attention to each one. As mentioned earlier, when you pay attention to the thoughts in your mind, you can reframe them. This will help you change the way you think. If you want to look at different tips and tricks that you can use to do this, look no further – this book has them all.

I hope the information in this book will help you become the master of your mind. Afterall, you're the only person that can declutter your mind and master your own thoughts. So what are you waiting for? You can start to improve your life today. You deserve it!

www.ingramcontent.com/pod-product-compliance
Lightning Source LLC
LaVergne TN
LVHW041626070526
838199LV00052B/3256